JESUS RECEIVE ME

IDENTITY. PURPOSE. DESTINY

EARLIN BLAIR

FIRST EDITION

(Paperback) 978-1-0686880-1-0

Jesus Receive Me is published by TC Publishing

For information, please direct emails to: info@tc-publishing.com

CONTENTS

DEDICATION

This book is dedicated to my late Sister Sandra Blackstock. I am thankful that she was tuned into heaven and that, gradually, she shared with me what needed to happen in order to unfold my identity and purpose and *destiny*. I am grateful for the constant encouragement and how she even found writing workshops to help me along.

Thank You, Father-God, for Your prompt to write this book.

To everyone who will read this book, thank you for spending your time on these pages. I extend blessings over your life, family, friends, and community.

ACKNOWLEDGEMENT

I extend my heartfelt gratitude to Tarnya Coley and TC Publishing for organising the Authors Breakfast and workshop sessions. These events have been truly inspirational, aiding in my progression and serving as a great source of motivation throughout the journey of creating this book. The experience has instilled in me a profound sense of achievement and a deeper understanding of the commission. God bless everyone involved.

Veronica Davis

FOREWORD

This book is valuable, especially for new Christians seeking God's will for their lives. God's call is often associated with calls to full-time ministry or as a missionary. Yet God uses ordinary people in extraordinary ways

Veronica and her late sister Sandra responded to God-given opportunities even within life's struggles and grew in faith and the knowledge of the Lord.

Sandra often requested Bibles to give to those she had spoken to or those she could help. Luke 16:10 reminds us how God tests our integrity in the small things. Her passion, enthusiasm and love for the lost were such an inspiration to others. In a relatively short time, she accomplished so much for God.

Both Veronica and Sandra welcomed opportunities to meet with others where they would receive Biblical teaching and training for evangelism. It is so [important to mix with those who will build you up and not those who will put out the fire.

This book illustrates the power of God-given dreams as God directly encourages and builds up His people. Be ready to share recurring dreams with God's people as you seek to decipher God's will.

In this book, we visit Jamaica, besides England. Have insights into Veronica's life such as sibling rivalry but see God preparing and equipping these women of God to respond to his call and fulfil their God-given destinies.
Be blessed- Be encouraged- Be challenged as you read this book.

There's a work for Jesus, ready at your hand

'Tis a task the Master just for you has planned

Hast to do His bidding, Yield Him service true;

There's a work for Jesus none but you can do,

Elsie D Yale

Rev Daryl Richardson BD ALBC BA MSc

INTRODUCTION

In unveiling these words, I recollect taking leave from my social worker team in 2017 to go on Jury Services. During the first week of the service, I went to sleep one night and heard this request: 'Leave work in a year's time and write a book.' It was in June 2018 that I realised that I needed to leave my employment. However, I continued to work until 2021, following COVID-19, when my sister Sandra went home to *glory*!

It became more urgent to write this book because Sandra had patiently encouraged me to discover my identity and purpose and destiny. She became my inspiration to finally take the leap.

Sandra was employed as a Community Support Worker and was loved and respected throughout the Manchester Community. In fact, she was well-known by the shopkeepers in Stockport, too. Sandra always had an engaging and encouraging grin for those she met. My sister was kind and helpful to the point of putting herself at a disadvantage.

This book takes me back to the glorious time I spent growing up in Jamaica. I have fond memories of being a child in the village and farming community there. Now, this translates into tradition in the UK, evolving families and culture.

Our vibrant young men and women who emigrated from Jamaica to various parts of the United Kingdom now have established roots in the UK through families, employment, community life, music, and language, which has integrated us as an extended Jamaican community.

For many years, we continued our collaboration with families in Jamaica, continuing the relationships that had been established long ago to forge lifelong connections to ensure future generations' survival.

When I look back now, life was 'sweet', but because we were all forging a life trail, the future was clouded with mist and required more unpacking to see where we were moving.

In growing up, there were certain questions I asked myself about life:
Has anyone born into this world had a feeling of total satisfaction with their accomplishments? Does money create happiness?

When you experience life challenges, how is it possible to recover sufficiently to return and forge a life that gives you some satisfaction?

The BIG ONE is: After having experienced a massive letdown in life by close personal caregivers, how can you recover and move forward successfully?

'Jesus, Receive Me' takes you on a journey from the Jamaican countryside and envelops you into a close relationship with Jesus, who was sent by His Father into this world to live like you and manage some of these issues from a human perspective.

Spiritual Blessings in Jesus Christ

[4] Even as he chose us in Him before the foundation of the
world, that we would be holy and without defect before Him
in love, [5] having predestined us for adoption as children
through Jesus Christ to Himself, according to the good
pleasure of His desire, [6] to the praise of the glory of His
grace, by which He freely gave us favour in the Beloved, [7] in
whom we have our redemption through His blood, the
forgiveness of our trespasses, according to the riches of
His grace. (Ephesians 1:4–7)

Compassionate One

Genesis 1:26: God said, "Let's make man in our image, after our likeness. Let them have dominion over the fish of the sea, and over the birds of the sky, and over the livestock, and over all the earth, and over every creeping thing that creeps on the earth."

Later in the garden, a mist arose from the earth and watered the whole surface of the ground. Then the Lord God formed man from the dust of the ground and breathed into his nostrils the breath of life, and Man became a living being. (Genesis 2:6–7)

The Man is Adam; he named everything. But there was no helper suitable for Adam. So, the Lord caused him to go into a deep sleep and took one of his ribs, which he made into Woman, and He brought her to the Man. Adam said, 'This is now bone of my bone and flesh of my flesh; she shall be called Woman, for she was taken out of Man.'

The Lord created humans to have fellowship with Him.

CHAPTER 1

ELFREDA – THE EARLY YEARS

Born in Jamaica, my mother Elfreda (Freda) Davis emerged into the community of St Elizabeth in August 1933. She was one of two children born to her mother, Nora, along with her brother Leonard. This dearly beloved brother formed and shaped Freda's life in a significant way that she could not have foreseen at the time of their birth.

Living in Jamaica brings with it connections that go back several generations, especially in the countryside villages, which comprise closely knit communities. This location is set against a high mountainous backdrop, with a view far into the distance of the Black River Town area, which is about an hour's drive from Round Hill, St Elizabeth.

Living in this tight-knit agricultural community, the family, along with Leonard and Freda, grew up farming their own area of land. As a teenager, when Leonard was offered a job on another farm, along with wages for his work, he thought this a brilliant earning opportunity, and embraced it. Leonard was so excited to be earning money that he thought about where he could secure these funds safely; management of his wages was critical.

Freda suggested that he might trust her to manage this with him. He promptly said, 'No!' Perplexed, Freda did not argue.

Leonard viewed his newly acquired profession with pride. He viewed a career in farming as a tremendous achievement.

'Where could be the safest place to put my money?' Leonard asked himself. He decided that he would put the money he had earned under a stone in one of the fields he tended. Leonard reasoned that since the fields were where he spent so much of his time, this would surely be the right place.

This was his first taste of his newfound freedom of earning and managing his money, and he wasn't aware of his other options. He rationalised that no one could know that the cash was there except him. So, he left for the night, settled in his mind that he had done the right thing.

When Leonard walked into the field the following day, he slowly lifted the stone to take out his money. His eyes widened. His mind screamed! He could not believe that there was no money there!

He stood there swaying as the gentle breeze brushed his body and his clothes flapped, confused as to why and what had happened. Shocked, his heart raced. Something transformational started to happen in those few moments to his whole being—his mind first, then his body and inner spirit. Leonard's initial responses unfolded as a cloud of devastation to his innermost being.

Freda knew her brother Leonard well and knew him to be immaculately presented. When this event happened, sanity lifted from him like a cloud, changing and erasing memories. From that moment onwards, he became a lost soul to her. When she encountered him, he was dishevelled and disorientated. He could not coordinate his thoughts to articulate language or communicate in conversation in any way that made sense. His organisational skills and emotions were non-existent; he was lost to her from that moment.

Freda watched in dismay. While her brother Leonard had a body, everything else had lifted from him like a cloud on the horizon when it disappears and is no more; the brother she knew had become someone who was unrecognisable to her in mind and body.

From that moment, Leonard became the community displaced person; he no longer related to Freda as his sister. Leonard began a nomadic existence in the region, sleeping in caves, where he prepared all his meals and managed all aspects of his daily life. Leonard moved around the lush countryside of St Elizabeth, selecting his camping sites at will. The freedom of his lifestyle meant that no one knew where he lived, but whenever he emerged, the community supported him with food and small amounts of money. At these times, the community reported sightings of him to interested families.

Leonard collected pieces of wood to build the fires he would use for cooking. Everything rotated around his fire, his sleeping area, and his clothes. He wore his clothes until they came to an end or were replaced with clothing gifts from his sister. However, when he received these gifts, he would sometimes sell them for a fraction of their value to buy food.

He never lived in a house with people again. Interestingly, his soul would still reach out for contact with the community. These people automatically cared for him, offering him food or allowing him to collect food from their fields. However, no one wanted him to stay on their land for too long because if he became ill, then he could become their responsibility.

Leonard was never to be Freda's brother again in the shape and form which they knew when they grew up together, loving each other. He could not make sense of life as it was lived nor articulate his views and feelings in the village culture anymore. Still, he sought company, and when passing the community 'meeting hub' on occasion, the locals would buy him a drink.

The community in which he lived always reported tales about Leonard's whereabouts, what they saw him doing, and when they saw him. His behaviour caused amusement among some of the locals; he'd grown 'strange', and people would smile in their contemplation of him.

When Freda caught phrases from people who found humour in some of the activities Leonard was engaged in, she was never amused because this was her beloved brother with whom she had grown up and knew so well. Freda loved him. From what she remembered, he was someone who was always careful about his life and appearance as he went out and about in the community; he was always immaculate and was known for this in the village.

Silently, Freda nursed the pain of loss in her heart and wondered at its intensity for her beloved brother. In those early years of their youth, she protected his image and character fiercely since she was the only one who knew him inside out. Her heart ached for him because he could no longer articulate this nor maintain their relationship. Yet, he was Freda's closest relative.

Devastated internally, Freda contemplated the cruelty of humanity because she felt strongly that someone had laid a trap for Leonard when he hid his money. It was a trap he only discovered when he returned to retrieve it the next day. It remained a mystery as to what really happened during those twenty-four hours that caused both their lives to change forever.

Meanwhile, Freda continued to work within the agricultural sector of the community. She also continued to hold Leonard in high esteem and related to him as the beloved brother she knew throughout their childhood.

Strangely enough, Freda never spoke with her family about their relationship as children and growing into adulthood. Instead, she focused on their 'here and now' existence and supported him with clothes and money at every opportunity.

These occasions would arrive when sightings of Leonard were reported. Freda would leave money or clothes and ask the person who had seen him to hand these things to him when they encountered him again.

Freda maintained a connection with their mother, and when she died, Leonard and Freda were both together. Their uncles were charged with managing their property and estate affairs. However, the uncles struggled and drank alcohol daily, which impacted their decision-making, and consequently, they were not able to manage the responsibility of the estate.

This was a dark wilderness season for Freda and Leonard because their uncles sold the estate and took the proceeds for themselves. Heartbroken, Freda was left with a massive hole in her heart; her mother had passed, and her beloved brother was unable to relate to the real world.

Freda's thoughts turned to the challenge of how she would manage for the future. She thought about this carefully and accepted an invitation to move into her cousin Lucille's home and manage all her affairs from there. Freda developed a very close relationship with her cousin Lucille and her mother, and they remained very close to Freda's heart throughout their lives.

Freda's strong sense of loyalty and independence fuelled her internally. She was empowered courageously for life's transitions and making history for herself and her family. She nursed the seed deep within her thoughts of moving to the United Kingdom. This dream started to grow inside her.

Throughout the time of support from Lucille and her mother, Freda became aware of how life-limiting alcohol could be if she took this path. Also, forgiveness started to shape her life for her uncles. This brought freedom to move in a direction which opened new opportunities for her to venture into. Consequently, life directed her towards the seed that was growing inside her and shaping her thoughts into leaving the island.

Romance in the Air

Freda continued to work within the community and eventually met a gentleman named Mortel Blair in the village while she was working on the farm. He lived with his parents, Frances (known as Sister Fanny locally), his sister Ellen, and Jacob (his brother), who were still living at home. They occupied a small one-room house that consisted of a bedroom and a kitchen for the whole family. Mortel was the youngest of the siblings, and with very little space in the family home, he decided to travel to America, where he was employed on farms. He travelled to several areas with the United States of America. While he was earning money in America, he asked his brother Jacob to oversee the building of his home on the same land near the original family home. Mortel returned to Jamaica to his new home and eventually met Freda. Their relationship developed, and it was not long before they produced a child, whom they named Veronica. However, this was a relationship not destined to bloom.

Mortel was the youngest male in his family, which was acknowledged to be a good family in the community. Mortel was known to many of the women in and around the area by reputation. He was a man who was known for catching the young women's eyes wherever he went.

Mortel was aware of his own strikingly handsome appearance; he had vibrant green eyes and a strong will and was well-presented among the locals. He was happy to engage with women romantically; however, this did not always mean he would accept responsibility for every child coming from their union.

The community was rural; therefore, when travelling in the area, Mortel would walk by most people's homes, and it was customary to stop and socialise at these times. Not surprisingly, many relationships started during these moments.

After some of these liaisons, a few women had the courage to speak up and present their children to him, and when he refused to acknowledge them, they took him to court for child support and acknowledgement. There were rumours of other children in the district, but most of the women stayed silent and merged their offspring into their existing families.

Sometimes, women would come out of obscurity to talk about past relationships. However, they would be met with a smile and nothing further. Mortel progressed into his senior years, and he did not give a hint of anything lurking in his past exploits. However, the residents who were old enough to live in the area around the same time as he did would allude to relationships privately.

As time went by, Mortel's vivid green eyes would become a mask for many hidden memories. He never spoke about his past and his female relationships. The only thing he would say was that the good Lord had blessed him, and he had used his blessings well during his lifetime. Then, he would give a gentle laugh.

Eventually, Mortel (known locally as Brother Mort) inherited the family land. His brother and sisters, who occupied the family home, moved to Kingston, Canada, and the USA as they developed their own relationships and marriages, and he continued farming there. Mortel's relationships led to him having nine children, which he acknowledged, loved and supported as well as he could.

After Mortel's time in America as a young man, he returned to Jamaica where he had built himself a beautiful pink two-bedroom house with a veranda and a tank in the yard that supplied a small community with drinking water and for general usage.

In the mountainous community where Mortel lived, there was a steep hiking trail on one side and a road for transportation, including taxis, on the other side. However, the road could become rough in places due to erosion from rainfall, making it essential to be familiar with the terrain for safe travel, both day and night. Mortel's house was situated on flat land nestled within the mountainside, with a forested ravine behind it extending down to the lower regions. The main crops grown here for sustenance included tomatoes, peanuts, grains, potatoes, and cassava.

Mortel, being the owner of his own land now, became self-employed, overseeing the management and production of the farm.He worked diligently on the land, making life work for himself and his family. He worked diligently on the land, making life work for himself and his family. Mortel had entered a new phase in his life, and he remained loyal to his partner and his family now.

As time passed, Mortel's life partner, Lydia Griffiths, played more of a role within the community and neighbouring farms. Their relationship developed, and Mortel proposed marriage on more than one occasion; however, because there were two families involved (Lydia was a widow who had children from her previous marriage), Lydia declined, preferring to maintain harmony and love for both families.

Lydia was the matriarch of the family and had the ability to infuse love into all parts of it. She found ways to spend time with individual members by catching them alone and building bonds securely to maintain the foundations of both families. Mortel and Lydia were well-known, loved, and respected within the region for many years. They became the joy, soul, and spirit of the community hub, forming links with history and customs forged through the generations.

Much later, when Veronica visited on holiday, both would share historical events of the families generationally. At that time, not many photographs were available, so the way to keep family history alive was to continually tell stories of the events. In those times, farming the land was the only available work in the country areas of Jamaica. Everyone who had land would plant crops, and whatever they cultivated could be sold locally or exchanged for other products. Everyone in the region had well-established relationships to confer with each other about what crops were being planned. When the planting season started, each person could sell locally first, and whatever was left could be taken to market.

CHAPTER 2

FREDA MAKING A NEW LIFE IN ENGLAND

During these times, many of the local women had lived within the farming community for years and had family connections that went back several generations. Although residents moved to other parts of the country in Jamaica, this did not happen frequently; hence, family links became stronger locally. These family ties could potentially cause complications for marriage prospects.

When Freda's cousin Lucille travelled to England, she invited Freda to join her. There was an increase in emigration developing within areas of the Caribbean to support England, the 'Mother Country'. England started to encourage locals with the promise of employment, providing opportunities and scope to broaden horizons. After all, it was the Mother Country, and it seemed like the most natural thing to do.

Freda travelled to England, where she met up with Lucille, who owned a home there. Freda moved in, and they supported one another during those early years in the UK.

The close family network that characterised their lives in the Caribbean transitioned to their newfound freedom in their new settings, and the connection and support continued developing within their culture and community.

Every day, they learned new details about their life in England. While walking through the streets, they saw signs in windows that read 'No Irish' or 'No Blacks'—a form of discrimination they had never encountered before. As new arrivals from the Caribbean, they realised that their adopted home presented unexpected challenges for them and their community.

In the homes of previous arrivals in the UK, where double beds were available, it was common for up to five people to share a bed each night. Despite the crowded conditions, everyone was grateful for a place to sleep and refrained from complaining, understanding from past experiences that this short-term arrangement was necessary during such times.

The early years in England formed the basis for their foundational education for survival; words like 'discrimination' started to shape their vocabulary. They did not understand why this was happening because while in the Caribbean, they spoke about the Mother Country with such affection and love. Now they were here, it was hard to understand this language.

This was a journey that many took in the early years after arriving at their destination, where this narrative shaped their new lifestyle as well as those of their children who were born there. However, many were vibrant young men and women and were able to enter into this transitional conversation in history enthusiastically.

They were being immersed in a culture that seemed impregnable for a young Jamaican; however, as a community engaging in conversations and employment, they started to shape their destiny within the country. Yet they were young, so jumping into the fire of culture was something they relished to shape their identity, purpose, and destiny, and through the symphony of opinions which sought to give meaning to their existence, they moved to the rhythm of the time.

They forged ahead, some marrying their childhood sweethearts and others finding wives within the local communities to which they now belonged. In the early days, the Caribbean community lived close together and socialised together. House parties were prevalent; it was not unusual to hear loud reggae music like Bob Marley singing 'One Love One Heart', booming, booming, booming out of homes during the evenings or weekends. At other times, people met in each other's homes to share stories, maintaining the legacy of storytelling to keep the home country alive and maintain strong family links.

Freda came from a close-knit community in Jamaica. Some places had the same family living on the same land for several generations. Needless to say, many were closely related, and people moving to other countries were a blessing because this would strengthen the family line.

After moving to the UK, Freda eventually met Valma Blackstock, who was originally from Clarendon in Jamaica. They developed a strong relationship that led to marriage, and they produced three beautiful children: Beverley, Trevor, and Sandra.

After moving to Manchester, Freda settled into the love of family life while establishing her independence. She eventually purchased her home with Valma (known as Slim) and moved there with their three children. They lived there for a number of years, and eventually, together, they decided to send for Veronica, who was still living in Jamaica with family and significant mother figures.

CHAPTER 3

VERONICA LIVING IN JAMAICA

Born in Jamaica on 27 October 1956, in the beautiful area of Bigwoods, Veronica was raised in the family home nestled in the grounds of a farm surrounded by mountains. When Veronica's mother moved to the UK when Veronica was three months old, this was an adventurous time of discovery when most residents were moving out into new ventures away from the island. Veronica lived with her father, Mortel, supported by her significant mothers, aunts, and uncles, while Freda travelled. In the early years, Veronica's care was split between Mortel and Mama Ida and Papa Sam. Occasionally, her Aunt Ellen and Uncle Jacob would have Veronica at their home overnight with their families.

At the time, many children in Jamaica lived within extended family networks while their biological parents moved to other countries to find a better life for them all. This pattern had been established within Veronica's family, and she moved between her father's home and her significant parents, which consisted of aunts and others who were close to her family.

Veronica loved to play outside every day. In Jamaica, daily life revolved around outdoor activities. Living on a farm, the adults tended to the land, planting various vegetables and short-term crops, like melons, that could be harvested in three months.

Veronica would make up her own games and build the associated toy to go with the character that fitted the part. These toys would be used repeatedly for play and hidden away on the farm at the end of the day. Children loved the games they invented and loved running around on the farm, indulging in the joy of creating and playing in the sunshine.

Curiously, those early years were challenging times for Veronica, but on reflection, the times were exciting for learning and developing in the natural outdoor environment. Veronica had never met her mother, although she often heard the adults referring to her. She knew that her mother was in England but, having no recollection of her or concept of what this meant, could not find any connection with these stories. Veronica merely received this information indirectly and knew that every so often, letters were exchanged between her father and mother, and money was sent from the UK to help support her.

Hiking up the Mountain

Papa Sam and Mama Ida, who played a significant role in Veronica's life, lived way up in the mountains of St Elizabeth in Round Hill. Their home was literally on the mountainside, and getting to their home meant hiking up the mountain, which was tough and invigorating. It involved navigating gullies, with gravel rolling down towards you while navigating the path up to their hillside home. Veronica loved this journey because it came with the promise of the delight of spending time in the loving company of Papa Sam and Mama Ida. She had incredible affection for them and would cry incessantly when she left for the shuttle between their home and her father's home.

In those times, everyone walked to most places because, living in a predominantly rural farming area, the landscape was surrounded by huge mountains and connected by dirt roads. The areas were accessible mainly by footpaths, so people had to be good walkers.

Growing up in the mountains exposed Veronica to the chance to explore the wilderness areas of the land, trees, and the rocky, hilly environment that she loved and connected with since she had a quiet and solitary nature. Living and moving outside during the days were wonderful ways to explore the land and feel the breeze brushing her skin, shaping and sweeping her into the life of the countryside.

Veronica was considered to be a fragile child, ready to cry at any little thing. Mama Ida kept saying: 'You have to toughen up.' She told Veronica that once she was in the UK, she would need a strong exterior to survive in that community.

Veronica would accompany Mama Ida and Papa Sam, doing jobs in the home and on the farm. She enjoyed being in the cornfields, breaking the corn, and reaping the yield for the home. They would frequently sit on the veranda, shelling beans that would later be cooked for dinner. Veronica loved these moments of doing tasks together. They would chat and laugh, especially when she was frightened when worms emerged from the bean shells, wriggling from the pods.

There was no electricity in those areas; at night, oil lamps provided light. Before that, they would sit out on the veranda, watching the sun disappear below the skyline. Then, a cacophony would rise from the bushes into the darkness; the gentle glow of the light from the lamps filled the hall and spilled into the night air on the veranda. In the bushes around the home, the crickets would chirp their song of creation, filling the air with tunes alongside their hidden neighbours. Love floated into the atmosphere of the darkness, making souls sing with joy. They would look up into the inky night sky and see the stars looking down at them.

On the veranda, Veronica kept a bottle that she used to catch fireflies and would keep them in the bottle through the evening. She used the light from the bottle to draw others as the night passed. The evenings were full of laughter, and there was a deep sense of fun and satisfaction. Before going to bed, they would release the fireflies from the bottle into the atmosphere, and they flew back into the night darkness.

Veronica had no idea that moving from the farming community in Jamaica and being thrust into city life could cause such inner confusion and massive culture shock. Ongoing and progressive adjustment in behaviour and connections would be a constant feature of life.

Veronica had a deep sense of feeling rooted in a close community that, until today, many of the country folks who moved into city life have felt, too.

No one even thought about the long-term effect of culture and community on their children's lives. These days, people are able to identify and link certain words to life experience.

Children who grew up in urban areas did not realise that those who moved from countryside farms would feel alien in cities.

Veronica had a great and deep affection for Mama Ida and Papa Sam. During their time together, they provided loving care for many years. This relationship continued after leaving the island through frequent contact through letters and return visits to their home on the island.

Lydia (Mama P) was a constant mother figure in the background, to begin with, and then as others moved off the stage, Lydia took centre stage and became the main mother figure. It's important to remember that Mama P had her own family from her first husband and later had three more children, who were Veronica's half-siblings. Mama P's loyalty was to her children from her first marriage and her immediate family with Mortel, who lived in the same household.

Lydia became a significant mother figure as she was Mortel's long-term partner for over 47 years; their children sealed that bond. For Veronica, it was a challenging time growing up in several families with different caregivers.

Veronica endeavoured to maintain and develop her relationship within each family network, but it remained incredibly challenging and confusing as to where her loyalty should lie.

Veronica did not have a guide for being a daughter in these relationships, and at times, would say the most inappropriate things because of wanting to create and protect her right to receive affection within the family circle. But how do you do that as a child, not having the perception, adult wisdom, and understanding to articulate this in words?

Veronica was confident in her father's love, and after moving to the UK, the bond became stronger because she travelled back with a view to maintaining the link by seeing family frequently. However, navigating several families as a stepdaughter is not an easy road to travel; it can get rough and bumpy at times.

Understanding relationships, communication, and connection as a child sitting in various families was a challenge; it was a 'wilderness' that Veronica had to courageously navigate, reflect on, and, where possible, create the pathway while travelling the journey. It's a little like a man walking through a jungle using a machete to chop away at bushes as he walks through the wilderness. What you find on those pathways might be those who want you to walk from their perspective, but you have to be determined to find your own path and dig in there until you are able to move forward safely with the knowledge you are forging your own trail.

CHAPTER 4

JOINING MOTHER IN THE UK

As mentioned, Mortel and Freda worked together through correspondence to manage the upbringing of their daughter. Both agreed to arrange a time for Veronica to move to join Freda in England. This happened in April 1967. On Easter morning, a 9-year-old Veronica landed at Manchester Airport. She had started her journey at Kingston Airport, then to the USA, and from there to London, where an air hostess took responsibility for ensuring that she reached her final destination. Veronica alighted, clutching her baby doll closely, assisted by the air hostess, and came face to face with her mother for the first time in her life as a child. There were just faces and names, and she was unable to recognise her mother. However, she was enveloped in a big hug by Freda and then introduced to her cousin Lucille.

Veronica travelled from the airport in bewilderment and, within hours, became part of a family of six, along with Slim, her stepfather. It was a strange sensation, and at the time, there were no words to explain the emotions, but she felt a little lost after coming from a small village and community within the Caribbean.

Arriving in the centre of the city of Manchester, everything seemed so bright, with lights everywhere, contrasting with the natural setting of rural Jamaica—the transition from countryside to city lights was overwhelming. Fortunately, the family lived in a terrace house, providing ample space.

During this time, with this extra accommodation, they were also able to let out spare bedrooms, earning some extra money from the property.

Veronica pondered the life opportunities she had been given thanks to her grandparents. Having arrived in the United Kingdom to meet her parents, she found them to be owners of their own accommodation, providing a platform for their grandchildren to build upon the legacy created by their grandparents and parents. It's important to acknowledge the inheritance passed down by our forefathers—the baton we must pass on to future generations.

Your Purpose and Destiny Can be Hidden

In Genesis 37–50, we see that Joseph, aged 17, was feeding the flock with his brothers. Now, his father loved him dearly and decided to make him a coat of many colours. When Joseph's brothers saw that their father loved him more, they hated him and could not speak to him with love. Joseph was a dreamer, and when he decided to share his dreams with his brothers, they hated him even more. He said to his brothers, 'Please listen. In this dream, we were bringing sheaves in from the field. All of a sudden, my sheaf rose up and stood upright, and your sheaves stood around it and bowed down to my sheaf.'

His brothers said to him, 'Will you really reign over us? Will you really have dominion over us?' Joseph's dreams and his words alienated his brothers further.

Then Joseph had another dream, and again he told it to his brothers, saying, 'I had another dream. The sun and moon and eleven stars were bowing to me.'

When he told his brothers and father, his father rebuked him and said to him, 'Will your mother and your brothers and I really come to bow down to you?'

Joseph went into the field with his brothers to work, not realising that they were plotting against him. His brothers debated killing him but instead sold him into slavery. It was then that his life purpose started to evolve and unravelled into his destiny. As Joseph progressed in his life, it was evident that he had God's blessing, and those around him recognised this. Hence, he was given responsibilities in order to reflect these blessings.

Things took a turn for the worse when Joseph was accused of rape. But again, his ability to interpret dreams came to his aid, and he eventually was released from prison when he was able to interpret the Pharoah's dream. In this dream, God had shown Pharaoh what He was about to do. Seven years of great abundance would come throughout all the land of Egypt. However, there would arise after them, seven years of famine. During this time, the abundance would be forgotten, and the famine would consume the land of Egypt.

Joseph's brothers eventually came to Egypt for grain because the famine forced them to buy grain there. When they arrived, initially, they came before the court to ask for assistance, but after two visits, they came face to face with their brother. At this stage, they were bowing to him in appreciation of the grain and assistance. The dream about the sheaves of corn had become a reality.

CHAPTER 5

INTEGRATION INTO FAMILY LIFE

While integrating into her new family, Veronica found that relationships evolved and developed progressively. However, a cloud of argumentative outbursts and turbulent waves characterised this family integration as the eldest child; Veronica became the first, Beverley second, followed by Trevor and Sandra when she arrived in the family. Trevor and Sandra were too young to understand what was happening. Sibling rivalry was unavoidable.

It was a constant fight, verbally. Again, this was another relationship challenge for Veronica as a child. The question that Veronica could not articulate at the time was: 'How does a child navigate communication in a new family that is clearly struggling with acceptance of this new sister? What eyes are they seeing me through, and how do they see me?'

Gradually, as the children grew up together, Veronica started to help around the home with household jobs.

To compound things, Veronica had a weak bladder, which, as a child, she was unable to control. She would play during the day, and at night, she would be so tired that she would sleep very deeply. Needless to say, most mornings when Veronica awoke, her bed was wet. In Jamaica, when this happened, her father would ensure that her bedding was washed and put out in the sun in the morning so it would be dry for the nighttime.

However, in the UK, it was cold and damp, so a wet bed posed a greater challenge. It had to be washed and put out for drying without the advantage of abundant sunshine. Not many people had washing machines then, so it was hard work when this happened daily.

In those times, no one understood anything about weak bladders and how this might impact a child's life; after playing during the day, it was hard to be up at night running to the bathroom. Veronica got a beating most mornings for wetting the bed until Mortel in Jamaica told Freda to send Veronica back there if she was going to continue with the beatings. The beatings stopped soon after.

Veronica loved her family in the UK, but the early years were a massive challenge. It was much like a moving kaleidoscope, a network of relationships that Veronica did not seem to have the skills to navigate intellectually or emotionally.

The family occupied a terrace house on Park Avenue in Longsight, Manchester; it was a six-bedroom house with a kitchen and bathroom. The street had a vibrant community of people who interacted with each other. Few understood at the time that this was being eroded by changes which were imminent; nor did they understand how valuable this was at the time.

CHAPTER 6

FIRE IN THE ATTIC

It was a cold winter morning, with snow high on the ground outside. At that time, these houses had no central heating except for the main fire in the kitchen and dining room, with oil lamps in other areas of the home.

These were lamps with kerosene oil poured in daily, or as necessary, and when lit, the flames shot up the central upper funnel area to the top, which was open; it was hot enough that it could be used to boil a kettle on it.

One morning, Veronica woke up shivering in the cold atmosphere and tentatively put her feet out of the bedding and onto the floor. Still shivering, she lit the lamp and stood near it to get warm. As the heat filtered up, she could feel the warmth on her legs easing the cold.

Suddenly, Veronica became aware that her nightdress was dangerously close to the lamp. Within seconds, the flames caught and lit the nightdress. Fuelled by the flimsiness of the material, the fire spread rapidly up the nightdress.

Veronica started screaming and shaking the lit area of her nightdress, jumping up and down. All this did was spread the fire more quickly!

Meanwhile, Veronica's sisters, Beverley and Sandra, were fast asleep in the double bed nearby, unaware of what was happening.

Veronica slept in a single bed with the cat at her feet; at this stage, the cat was long gone. Her stepfather Valma

(Slim), who was downstairs in his bedroom with Veronica's mother, ran up the stairs and burst into the room, quickly putting the fire out.

By this time, the fire had burnt the whole of Veronica's stomach area, and the skin started to strip off. The incident seemed so unreal, strange, and surreal for Veronica. It was as if no one knew whether this was real or what the best course of action was. In shock, everybody seemed to move in slow motion, unsure of what to do next.

Freda decided to take Veronica to Lucille's home, and upon arrival, it was determined that Veronica needed urgent medical attention. An ambulance was called, and Veronica was taken to the children's hospital.

After arriving at the hospital, Veronica underwent an examination, during which the consultant decided that admission was necessary. This turned into a lengthy stay. Over the following weeks, it was uncertain whether Veronica would survive, given the severity of the burns. She was placed in an isolation bed and fed milky fluid every hour. Nothing else was given during those early days.

Veronica was in the hospital for approximately six months. She relied solely on milk for sustenance, administered multiple times daily by nurses, while she spent most of her time sleeping. She remained hospitalised for several months, to the point where she was unable to walk upright because the healing of the skin on her stomach restricted her freedom of movement.

Progressive healing, supported by rehabilitation in the ward and the loving care of family and staff, restored Veronica's mobility. However, the period of hospitalisation and the severity of her wounds meant Veronica needed more time for recovery, particularly since agitation in the affected area exacerbated the problem. This led to Veronica spending an extended period in Wales for rehabilitation. Here, she gently recuperated over eight weeks, which allowed her to return home to the important business of growing up. However, she still needed much more support as the healing created itching throughout the area.

Following this initial phase, Veronica had follow-up aftercare from the hospital for about five years for skin grafts. Over the period of one week and then progressively over the years, Veronica underwent skin grafts from her legs to her stomach to restore some normality in that area.

The accident with the fire happened quite soon after Veronica's arrival in the United Kingdom from her native Jamaica, and it had a profound impact on her life. Within her home environment, balancing education and adjusting to the new culture on top of this new challenge left life in turmoil.

Veronica found herself navigating this new challenge while still under the protective shelter of her family, but she felt adrift, unable to grasp the direction her life was taking amidst the haze of uncertainty.

Initially, Veronica's family and friends empathised with what she had gone through and understood what she was learning to deal with. However, as life unfolded within the family home, the memory of the event faded. Her injuries were not visible, so the incident was gradually forgotten, which was perhaps a good thing. However, for Veronica, the event held significant personal meaning, and coping with life's challenges became a private battle, viewed through the lens of what Veronica had been learning and experiencing since her arrival in the UK.

Outwardly, there was no sign of the accident, so people focused on Veronica without assuming it had impacted her life opportunities. She did not perceive any stigma attached to what had happened and did not feel the need to draw attention to her past injuries, except during medical appointments where the scars would be seen.

Here again, as a child, Veronica questioned how to cope with this massive change in her life. She moved within the rhythm of the times, allowing the orchestration of life voices to direct the flow of her learning in education, culture, and developing friendships with new people. Strangely, Veronica did not think she had the capacity to learn much because of the many challenges in her short life, such as hospital admissions for treatments.

CHAPTER 7

CAREER ENGAGEMENT — THE FUTURE

Transitioning into employment and integrating into the community presented significant challenges for a Jamaican family living in the United Kingdom compared to their tight-knit community back in Jamaica. Seeking familiarity, Veronica's mother, Freda, had found comfort and support among women from her Jamaican culture, and they remained close friends throughout their lives in England. This bond was especially strong with families who had lived nearby in their communities in Jamaica.

Cousin Elleston was one of the people who visited the family home frequently when he came to the UK. In conversations with Freda, they recalled stories of their earlier years, and they would laugh and talk incessantly about funny events that had happened in their earlier years. They would spend hours sipping tea and eating snacks, relaxing in laughter and musings.

In the background, the children would overhear them and marvel at their conversation because sometimes they would speak over each other in excitement, recalling these events with exuberance. It was hard to tell who was listening to whom. Yet nothing seemed lost in translation; both knew that they were sharing cherished moments. Later, the family would joke about this with Freda. They loved this time together and chatted about the old days in Jamaica and how their youth was filled with such fun and laughter. Their chatter filled the atmosphere of the home with warmth and joy.

Veronica healed sufficiently to attend secondary school, but these were days that did not produce much in terms of educational achievement. This was largely because her scars were constantly itching, which had the effect of distracting her during the school day. When Veronica left school, she could hardly read. To resolve this, she decided to go to night school. Initially, this was to catch up on her education, but ultimately, learning became something that shaped her whole life. Some friends would jokingly ask her mother if Veronica was going to go to night classes all her life.

Veronica opted to work in a catalogue company, initially as a telephonist, dealing with queries and complaints. She attended night school at the same time to gain the qualifications needed for advancement in her career. Veronica soon realised that the wages she was earning as a single woman were not enough to live on and be independent. This, of course, posed questions and challenges as to how to move ahead. Discovering that financial instability could lead to vulnerability was a frightening realisation. The inability to earn enough to cover expenses like bills and rent, as well as essential living necessities, posed a significant threat to independence.

CHAPTER 8

GENTLE DESTINY PROGRESSION: THE CALL

During her childhood years, Veronica and her siblings graduated from attending house parties to being introduced to the local church's children's Sunday school, where Veronica was taught from the King James Bible about how Adam was created by God, who introduced him to the Garden of Eden. God later presented Adam with his wife, Eve. Together, they were given instructions about managing their home and the fruit trees available to them in the Garden. Specific instructions were given not to eat from one tree.

Genesis 1:26–28 (the creation of man in the image of God):
26 God said, 'Let's make man in our image, after our likeness. Let them have dominion over the fish of the sea, and over the birds of the sky, and over the livestock, and over all the earth, and over every creeping thing that creeps on the
earth.' 27 God created man in his own image. In God's image,
He created him; male and female, He created them. 28 God
blessed them. God said to them, 'Be fruitful, multiply, fill the earth, and subdue it. Have dominion over the fish of the sea, over the birds of the sky, and over every living thing that moves on the earth.'

The children started attending church as a family with their mother, whom, over time, they can reflect and say God met powerfully as she maintained her time in prayer and abiding in the Word of God, according to John 15:4: 'Abide in me, and I in you.' Gradually, Veronica responded, and at the age of 14, she felt that she needed to say yes to inviting Jesus into her life. Looking back, Veronica did not experience a massive, earth-shaking moment. She knew that God was ushering her into His Kingdom for His love and protection. In John 6:44, the Bible does state that no one comes to Jesus unless he has been called by the Father.

Veronica woke up to the Wisdom and Knowledge that was blowing in the winds her way from the Gospels, and over a number of days and weeks, felt strongly that this was something she was being called to do. The challenges she was encountering at the time propelled her into the security of Jesus' arms for His love and protection to embrace her under His wings. Psalm 91:1 'He who dwells in the secret place of the Most High...'

Within the church community, there were other mothers who had children of a similar age, and together, they formed a youth group. They learned from one another, honouring and supporting each other by organising events, visiting each other's homes, and sharing meals, love, and laughter. They grew together in their understanding of unconditional love and shared the Word of God with each other. They also grew in their skills and knowledge, loving God as a Friend and Saviour, and out of these relationships, a deeper connection.

Those who could sing followed this as their designated calling, purpose, and destiny in their lives. While they were unsure how this would relate to their employment, this unfolded later. One of the members, Vida, initially became the Youth Leader and was instrumental in pointing the others towards a fruitful development routine in their lives. Eventually, Veronica became a Youth Leader supported by Vida and was thrown into the work of delivering leadership, engaging the group in collaborative discussions to arrange activities and complete tasks.

Looking back, those were amazing times; everyone was enthusiastic every step of the way and very innovative in creating opportunities. They planned local events and frequently met at each other's homes for Bible study. Other times, they would travel to Leicestershire for Youth Conventions, where other young people attended. It was a great time for worshipping, singing vibrantly, and just lifting up the name of Jesus in Worship. These were amazing experiences in the atmosphere of loving God and growing up.

Those times, as young women and men, went on to shape their destinies. It was an environment that allowed full self-expression. Everyone flourished in their learning in a place where it was safe to make mistakes and not be judged. Nobody was ever negative or obstructive about others' growth and development.

Veronica taught Sunday School, which was a great confidence booster, and she was allowed to speak to everyone, which was called 'exhortation'. This was also the building block for Veronica's relationship in God, a communion time which initiated a willingness to engage in a deeper relationship with God as He offered it. This was foundational and was maintained through daily devotions, and walking in the garden and chatting with Father-God to maintain a friendship.

The church community became a huge ground for imparting skills that would launch these young people beyond the church walls and into their future careers. These abilities complemented the education they received in formal institutions. Since many educational establishments were just getting used to teaching children of diverse backgrounds, they sometimes found it difficult to see the potential of each individual beyond their outward behaviour.

Ephesians 1:3–6: [3] Blessed be the God and Father of our
Lord Jesus Christ, who has blessed us with every spiritual
blessing in the heavenly places in Christ, [4] even as He
chose us in Him before the foundation of the world, that
we would be holy and without defect before Him in love,
[5] having predestined us for adoption as children through
Jesus Christ to Himself, according to the good pleasure of
His desire, [6] to the praise of the glory of His grace, by which
He freely gave us favour in the Beloved.

Freda started to attend church and was powerfully impacted by God, and progressively, she found that she was able to speak with individuals about their longer-term destiny calling in God. The home was filled with prayers daily; wherever anyone was within the home, they could hear their mother praying. This echoed around the house most days, filling the atmosphere with the love of the Messiah. Veronica would fondly recall the sound of her mother singing her favourite song: 'Prayers of heaven how sweetly they ring; ringing a message unto Jesus our King, when you are burdened with troubles and care, just ring on and on and He will answer your prayer!'

Freda's love for God was so amazing; it seemed that she prayed night and day sometimes. This was because she saw every opportunity as a moment to spend in God's presence.

Veronica loved being in the church environment, as it was a lively and active place where individuals would shout, 'Hallelujah! Hallelujah!' at different intervals.

Like the children of Israel, there is an inheritance awaiting us when we arrive at Jesus' feet. But we do not sit at Jesus's feet for his gifts; we are there to worship in relationship and intimacy. In Luke 10:38–42, Mary and Martha depicted this in their relationship with Jesus.

38 As they went on their way, He entered into a certain village,
and a certain woman named Martha received Him into her
house. 39 She had a sister called Mary, who also sat at Jesus'
feet, and heard His word. 40 But Martha was distracted with
much serving, and she came up to Him, and said, 'Lord,
don't you care that my sister left me to serve alone? Ask

her therefore to help me.'[41] Jesus answered her, 'Martha, Martha, you are anxious and troubled about many things, [42] but one thing is needed. Mary has chosen the good part, which will not be taken away from her.'

This relationship was evident with Freda, who had gifts, but Veronica did not hear it clearly at the time because she was still developing. She just wondered how it was that her mother could seem to know what she had been doing in the bedroom the previous day, when the door was closed and locked. The gift and the power of prophecy started to emerge in the family home and church community; however, people referred to this as 'noise'. No one seemed to have any frame of reference or understanding of what was happening.

Upon reflecting and discussing with others who were present at the time, Veronica was surprised to realise that her mother's utterances were indeed prophetic. She now understood that the prophetic gift had begun to manifest in their home. It was remarkable because her mother would observe situations and make comments that would later unfold exactly as she had spoken. This phenomenon continued to develop over the years.

CHAPTER 9

MOVEMENT INTO CULTURE

In the UK, the family gradually immersed themselves in the culture of the educational systems, the general society culture, and the church culture, which was exceptionally challenging at times.

They also had their Caribbean culture, which was there underneath all these new ones. This was like wearing several layers of clothing and having to be conscious of which one was relevant depending on the occasion. In referring to culture, part of this relates to language, food, and music, which orchestrates the rhythm of life.

In Jamaica, Veronica's family was accustomed to growing their own food on the farm. They grew grains and cassava, which were readily available to them. When the cassava was fully matured, they would harvest it, peel off the skin, and grate it into a bowl. Then, they would press it overnight to remove the milky juice. In the morning, after taking it off the press, they would empty the contents into a basin, producing a lovely white flour.

This flour was used to make 'bammy bread', which was the accompaniment for eating with meat or grains. Many of their ancestors grew up on this diet because there was no bread in those days. Additionally, they grew sweet potatoes and various other crops. Yams were also grown in the hilly areas near where they lived.

What was an interesting challenge was the fact that many who emigrated from the agricultural farming areas moved directly to city life in the UK. Today, several generations have this heritage, but many children are not familiar with this dramatic change that impacted their parents' lives. Moving and having a family and developing as adults in this new culture, their way of life must have created many emotional challenges, which at times were not articulated. Perhaps they were not even aware of them because they were busy immersing themselves in the community and meeting the daily needs of their families.

The remote villages within the Caribbean were the most amazing places to live and grow as a child. Veronica appreciated this later; however, growing up, she really did not have the capacity or language for the many changes which were continually unfolding. Leaving her father and moving to her significant family network around Jamaica and then moving to the United Kingdom to live with her mother and her new family caused a lot of upheaval.

At the age of 17, having left full-time education and starting to attend night classes, Veronica gradually filtered through the various jobs which she thought might be suitable. This was the point at which she found a post as a telephonist at a catalogue company, as mentioned previously. She would address enquiries when individuals placed orders initially, and if, during the course of waiting, an issue developed, the company could be contacted to chase this up.

Veronica was employed at the catalogue company for 16 years until, due to a multiple redundancy proposal, it became necessary to contemplate moving on again. At this stage, Veronica had acquired several GCSE qualifications, including English Language, Civil Law, Economics, and Religious Education, while attending night classes. This enabled her to make an application to start the University of Manchester's Social Work course.

In fact, Veronica applied to both the Polytechnic education centre, and Manchester University and was accepted at both. She was really excited but had the dilemma of choosing one. Have you ever doubted that you might make the cut for something, then you are offered both options, and you are confounded by the problem of having to make a choice? Veronica considered the fact that she would probably not have any extra money during her time studying, so she chose the one nearest to her home.

It was an amazing time for Veronica. University is never what you imagine it will be; the atmosphere depends on the town in which the university is located, the staff there, the culture within the university, and the curriculum for the duration of your time there. Additionally, there are opportunities for creative collaboration and engaging discussions within groups.

Veronica had helpers in making these decisions around her studies, one of whom was a gentleman who worked within the catalogue company. After observing Veronica for many months within the company, one day, he approached her and suggested that it might be worth her while to attend university and perhaps move into a career of her choice. Veronica's sister Beverley had just completed her training at university, which also influenced Veronica's decision to change her direction and find her life identity and purpose. This was the road that would eventually lead to the destiny that had begun with her ancestors.

After going to university, Veronica believed strongly that every child should have the opportunity to attend university. The experience really opened her up to so many sets of principles, life opportunities, and the ability to take risks. It prepares a person for life and living independently within different cultures. She was grateful for the opportunity to develop her skills and abilities further.

Drawing on her experiences thus far and considering her mother's recent passing in 1990, Veronica felt a strong leaning towards Social Work for her long-term career. This came from a deep-rooted situation within her family, and Veronica wanted to test whether this choice would give her the pathway in life's journey to wisdom. Gradually, embracing forgiveness and nurturing love will unlock the potential for healing and growth in her life, continuously fostering inner peace and joy. She chose the relevant courses at Manchester University to fit this job specification, took proactive steps to achieve her goal, and completed the application process. Subsequently, Veronica was invited to an interview, which she anxiously attended. Upon receiving an offer of admission from the university, she was ecstatic to have reached this significant milestone.

Veronica's university years were challenging as well as productive, and she always viewed her career choice as the right decision for her. Amidst the transition and studies following her mother's death, she found comfort in the knowledge and insights gained during her university education, particularly in processing the emotions of grief and loss associated with the passing of her mother.

Some of the subjects in the training were closely related to real-life situations, often striking a nerve. Yet in another way, it was the most exhilarating time of her life because several elements came together to shape her future. Having spent many years in jobs that did not challenge or create a sense of achievement, this became a welcome interjection into Veronica's life's progression.

This period unveiled a traumatic time in Veronica's life because her mother was the first member of her close family to exit this world. Freda had retired back to Jamaica, which had always been their plan to make a better life for themselves and return 'home'. Veronica was totally devastated by her loss, and it became a roller-coaster time as she dealt with grieving. There were times when Veronica felt like she was dragged to the bottom of the ocean by her emotions and then bubbled up to the surface again to recover some equilibrium, both emotionally and physically.

In 1986, Veronica went into adult social work. At that time, it was a challenging area to work in—it still is, especially since the emergence of COVID-19 in 2019, which has impacted many cultures around the world.

Social work opened up a new world of meeting adults who were living their lives with various challenges. Since these were adults, many had retired with a range of physical health conditions, like stroke, dementia, mental health conditions, and alcohol issues, to name a few.

Many individuals were seen in their homes, which required Veronica to conduct assessments there, speaking to them about their understanding of their situation, and completing documentation relating to that person. Over the years, Veronica found that meeting individuals imparted many life stories of successful accomplishments and well-lived lives. However, when faced with certain health challenges, these individuals had to find new ways to manage their lives, either by accepting their circumstances or seeking new solutions.

The foundational principles that were observed were person-centred, so no two people were the same, even though they may have had the same condition. Working with individuals was engaging, and for Veronica, coming from the background of living in the Word of God, this meant that love featured highly in the way she addressed and characterised her life around individuals. Furthermore, she discovered that much of the terminology that was used originated from the New Testament Bible, which speaks about 'unconditional positive regard' and refers to ways of loving and treating individuals in the world.

Veronica later read through the whole Bible and found that the court system shares similarities with the accounts from Exodus onward. Here, the foundation for the Ten Commandments is laid, with each commandment further elaborated in subsequent chapters, forming the foundation of civilisations at the time of the merging of generations and kingdoms.

So, human relationships depicted in the Community of the Bible seem to mirror current society. Through this exploration, Veronica learned to love Jesus Christ more and more through everything she did. She did not need to tell people what her belief was because her behaviour and attitude were the carriers of this message.

The field of social work is a place where so many different characters come into play, and as Veronica progressed along her life journey, she found that individuals started to point her in the direction of her destiny, even though they were not aware that they were doing it. This is what it means to live in the Word of God and in line with the person of the

Holy Spirit, who is in us. John 15:4 says, 'Abide in me, and I in you.' The Word of God—to abide means to remain and dwell—continued to form the foundational support for her decision-making. John 15:26 states, 'When the Comforter is come, whom I will send unto you from the Father, even the Spirit of Truth, which comes from the Father, He shall testify of me.'

Veronica sometimes heard individuals identifying special skills in her that were not obtained within the social work arena; others said things like 'someone with a name like your name is destined for something greater than social work.' Veronica heard this like a prophecy over her life, and she grew to accept it with gratitude. Veronica's relationship within her work community became well-established, and she enjoyed working with people from many different backgrounds and cultures. Although there were challenging moments, working together and sharing skills for development provided strong support. The environment became fertile grounds for growth in maintaining skills and empowerment. Veronica was thankful for the opportunity to meet individuals who were willing to share their life's achievements and challenges.

During this time, Veronica was still attending church; however, after her mother died, she struggled to remain the same person in her commitment to God. Times had become so turbulent for her that she thought she no longer had a smooth road to travel in her relationship with God. Veronica started to drift away from her regular attendance at church until she was going just two times a year. Eventually, her relationship and communion with Father-God stopped; she no longer prayed, and her relationship seemed to have ended. However, dreams started.

Around this time, Veronica began having dreams, especially of close family members. The dreams showed her the church community she attended and the hospitality section filled with people laughing and chatting. On two occasions, specific church sisters—Vida and Pat—were shown to her in her dreams. These were people she knew from her previous attendance. She saw both over the heads of others, walking towards her with beaming smiles to welcome her. As she opened the door and walked in, there was a flurry of activity. Veronica knew which church community this dream referred to and felt she needed to visit there.

CHAPTER 10

EXPLOITS IN JAMAICA

Veronica had decided that she needed to start attending her church community; however, due to a planned holiday, she opted to have her holiday first. Having arrived at Kingston Airport in Jamaica, she was met and escorted to her brother Colin's home. Veronica originally lived in Jamaica and had family in several areas. She decided it would make sense to travel to visit relatives first, then settle and enjoy the rest of the time in Kingston. Veronica travelled to Round Hill, St. Elizabeth, by taxi, and her brother Prince agreed to meet her there. Her journey was filled with nostalgia and excitement as she reconnected with her roots and family members.

During her visit, one of Veronica's nephews, Oshane, came around for the evening, gathering with other family members who came by. In the cool of the night, they looked up at the night sky, which was pitch-black, with stars glittering in all directions. This was reminiscent of Veronica's childhood, when she grew up in the countryside. Veronica loved the whole ambience of the family and the atmosphere that enveloped them while she was there.

During this time, one of Veronica's nephews related a story about a heavyset man who fell asleep while sitting on a white plastic chair on his veranda. While he was sleeping, the chair collapsed, and the legs broke, and the man went down heavily and damaged his back. At that moment, for some reason, this story resonated with Veronica as she sat and listened; deep down inside, she knew that the next place she was planning to visit and stay the night also had those white chairs.

The following morning, Veronica left for her aunt's home, which was her next family destination. On arrival at the marketplace in Mandiville, Veronica waited a long time to be met by her family. When the family member arrived, they caught a taxi, stopping at the bank, before travelling to her home. When Veronica arrived at her aunt's home, her aunt started cooking the evening meal. Veronica sat on a white chair in the doorway adjacent to the kitchen. This chair was just like the one that had been described the previous evening. She listened to her aunt, who was chatting away with her and moving around the kitchen to collect ingredients for the dish.

Suddenly, the legs of the chair broke underneath Veronica. This prompted an immediate strategic response from Veronica because she had the memory of the life-saving information fresh in her mind from the previous night. Veronica managed to support herself and pressed back against the wall so she would not go down with the chair. Veronica was thankful to her nephew, who had brought to mind the story of the man who had fallen asleep on his chair.

Veronica's aunt continued moving about in the kitchen, and when Veronica told her what had happened, she reacted angrily, which was strange. She said in an accusing tone that Veronica had put too much weight on the chair and said it was her fault it broke. But Veronica did not know what was to come!

A family member warned Veronica that a man might appear later that evening, so she should not worry. When she went to sleep that night, her aunt deliberately woke her up every hour. Veronica was unsure why her aunt was doing that. She was perturbed by this behaviour and wondered whether her aunt was trying to get her to extend her stay. However, she was set to return to Kingston the next day.

When Veronica was getting ready to leave the next morning, her aunt asked, "Did you have a good rest last night?" This struck Veronica as strange because she had been called frequently throughout the night, leaving her confused about what was happening.

As she set out to travel back to Kingston, her aunt still wanted to keep her there longer. A taxi, which could have taken them to Mandeville town centre, was declined by her aunt, who sent it away, saying it did not travel in the direction they needed. Eventually, another taxi came, and the driver knew her. When Veronica's aunt tried to send him away, he insisted that he could take her to the location she needed and would not be persuaded to leave them. The taxi driver said, 'Get in,' and closed the door.

This incident reminded Veronica of how awesome God is and how he knows all our moves, even though, at that time in Jamaica, Veronica was not clothed in the Righteousness of God. She would only come back under his wings in the Body of Christ when she returned to the UK (Psalm 91).

Jesus Christ can see way ahead of us and knew this event would happen. He started to give Veronica dreams that would eventually lead her back to Him, thereby committing her life fully back to Him and becoming a part of the fellowship. God wanted her to commit her life to Him, and by being in His presence and in relationship with Him, He could start the work of her restoration into the Kingdom. An example of this is the Samaritan Woman—Jesus knew she would be coming to the well for water:

John 4:4–7 (The Samaritan Woman. True Worshipper of Jesus
Christ): 4 He needed to pass through Samaria. 5 So He came
to a city of Samaria, called Sychar, near the parcel of ground
that Jacob gave to his son, Joseph. 6 Jacob's well was there.
Jesus, therefore, being tired from His journey, sat down by
the well. It was about the sixth hour. 7 A woman of Samaria
came to draw water. Jesus said to her, 'Give me a drink.'

During the visit to Jamaica, Veronica stayed with her brother Colin in Kingston. One morning, she woke up, and the word 'when?' formed on her lips and in her spirit. This surprised Veronica greatly, but she soon realised she was being asked: 'When are you coming back to me, Veronica' More importantly, she was being asked when she was going to come into the Kingdom. God will not force you into the Kingdom; He will ask you and await your agreement and full commitment to Him.

This materialised as an expression in Veronica's consciousness. She was utterly delighted and amazed that God was indeed having a conversation with her. She sat on her bed, smiling at the incredible nature of God.

What she did not realise at that moment was the urgency. It was only when she returned to the UK and faced a terrifying sequence of events but was advised not to feel or show fear that the matter became urgent for her. What is incredible about this is the way God walks with us, even at times when we have moved away from Him, and continues to woo us back into the fold of love and communion.

Once back in the UK, the world that Veronica had known prior to leaving was no more. In fact, events had overtaken her through her connection with a family member in the Caribbean. The family member, who was deeply involved in 'darkness', gave her personal details to a person to transfer dark activities from her to Veronica. But here God had it covered, as seen in Psalms 23: 'When you walk through the valley of the shadow of death, I am with you.' He even allows us to sit at the table to feast with the enemy; again, He is with us there.

Veronica recounted the information to her sister Sandra about what had transpired during her visit on holiday. This started a life-changing journey of walking Veronica into her true identity, purpose, and destiny.

Sandra supported Veronica and took her to her fellowship group, and then to two other churches and said that these were her choices for returning to the Church community. However, because Veronica had dreams about the church she originally attended, she decided that was the direction to follow. Veronica returned to her church and joined a small, intimate prayer group, which was excellent for spending time in prayer.

Now, Sandra attended the Elim Pentecostal Community Church, and thankfully, she was able to pray for Veronica there and speak with experienced believers. The Lord started to show Sandra how to progressively and gradually walk with the Person of the Holy Spirit, and direct Veronica through 'warfare to Deliverance' according to God's Words. In the early stages, Sandra gave Veronica some emergency strategies to manage the situation when she was woken up by demons which were transferred by the family member, usually during the night.

Later, Sandra arranged to meet with her at a cafe in Stockport. On her arrival, Sandra took out three small books, which she suggested that Veronica read, adding that they could be read quite quickly. In one of the books, Sandra took Veronica through a few sections and asked her to read them. Then she asked Veronica what she remembered. Clearly, Sandra was demonstrating how Veronica's mind could be impacted by everything that had happened.

Sandra explained that Veronica would need to know the Scriptures like Jesus did when he was led by the Spirit into the wilderness. At that time, when a dark presence could be sensed in the room. Veronica would pull the bedding over her head and hide beneath the covers, but Sandra was adamant that she had to address situations as they arose, responding in the Power of the Holy Spirit quickly and boldly.

The Scriptures detailed the 'boldness' employed by the Disciples in Acts when the Apostle Paul prayed to enable believers to operate under the anointing of the Holy Spirit without fear. Sandra showed Veronica how easily the Word of God could be taken away from a person, as in the Parable of the Sower. So, she had to work specifically knowing the work and Word of God in a way that entered her world, like 'Abide in the Word' (John 15:4), which led to being deeply rooted (Psalm 1), so the Holy Spirit could retrieve these when needed to equip her during times of combat to use in battles.

In 2016, while this crisis was erupting, Sandra asked Veronica if they should visit Israel; there was a trip being planned by Lighthouse Church. Veronica automatically responded and said yes, thinking that they might never get there. She did not give the suggestion serious consideration at the time because so many things were happening in her life. However, as the year unfolded, they started to plan at intervals, and they put money away for the visit.

Sandra and Veronica eventually travelled to Israel, alighting at Tel Aviv Airport. There, they were met by a gentleman who resided in the country and had connections with those in the area they would visit, eventually. They were new to this type of travel, which was a little like a Pilgrimage to where Jesus Christ was born. It was an exciting time for them and a respite from all that was happening back at home.

They had never had family holidays together, so it was special to have this time. However, it was not evident to them how special this would be until COVID-19 appeared around the world, and Sandra was taken from the family in the second wave of the infection.

Veronica and Sandra travelled with eleven other women and one gentleman, a Pastor and husband to one of the ladies. It was their wedding anniversary, so this was an incredible time for them both.

Veronica paid tribute to Sandra because, without her love, patience, and willingness to submit her life to God so He could use her in this special way, it would have been almost impossible for Veronica to progress. When Veronica approached her friends in the bookshop, she shared what happened on holiday. They were frightened by what they had heard. This would have meant that Veronica would not have been able to walk the road because it was scary and lonely. However, with God and her sister, Veronica never felt alone.

Sandra had amazing courage, and Veronica continued to be thankful for her life every day. Sandra was taken from the family during the height of COVID-19 on 15 January 2021. She put up an amazing fight, but there were too many battles for her to overcome, and she moved on to be with Jesus. Yet, she still came back to whisper to Veronica, 'Let me go' and 'You are supposed to be a teacher.'

This amazing confirmation of Veronica's destiny came during her early years as a Sunday school teacher. During her employment, she trained approximately six university students who came to the office on placements. However, Veronica was uncertain about her skills and abilities. She acknowledged now that she loved teaching students, although at first, she was reluctant to engage in this area of work.

Interestingly, Veronica found that she possibly loved teaching as much as social work. It was really interesting watching students progress from arriving to quickly building a high level of skills. Veronica thought with deep satisfaction that it was brilliant to see that development. These achievements were what she wanted to see in her life. No matter what you might experience, it is worthwhile to chart a pathway for your own personal story to unfold.

CHAPTER 11

INHERITANCE — JESUS, RECEIVE ME

Psalm 115:15–16

May you be blessed by the LORD, the Maker of heaven and earth. [16] The highest heavens belong to the LORD, but the earth he has given to mankind.

John 1:1

In the beginning was the Word, and the Word was with God, and the Word was God.

Veronica learnt that Father-God loves us according to His Words in the Bible. He has no favourite. They are powerful enough to accompany us through the darkest valley, the deepest wilderness and the worst times of our lives. These times can feel like they're never-ending, but God gives us hope, and the momentum in His words propels us to this goal.

Psalm 91:1–2 states: He who dwells in the secret place of the Most High I will rest in the shadow of the Almighty.
[2] I will say of Yahweh, 'He is my refuge and my fortress; my God, in whom I trust.'

In a place of *joy* and rejoicing, He is our refuge and hope, too.

Just like when the disciples were in the boat, they called out to Jesus (Matthew 8:23–27):

[23] When He got into a boat, His disciples followed Him.

24 Behold, a violent storm came up on the sea, so much
that the boat was covered with the waves; but He was
asleep. 25 The disciples came to him and woke Him up,
saying, 'Save us, Lord! We are dying!' 26 He said to them,
'Why are you fearful, O you of little faith?' Then he got
up, rebuked the wind and the sea, and there was a great
calm. 27 The men marvelled, saying, 'What kind of man
is this, that even the wind and the sea obey Him?'

God equips us to walk through the valley. It does not mean that we will not experience challenging times, but what it means is that Jesus will 'jump in the boat' with us to ride out the storm together. He expects us to stay in the boat with the knowledge that He is with us, giving us the wisdom, knowledge, and strength to move through the experiences. As you evolve through these times, you will have self-doubt, but the Word of God provides the sure foundations to stand in His Victory.

On reflection, Veronica read through biography in the early years of her life to see whether individuals were having happy and fulfilled lives. This showed many were unhappy even when they had all the money they wanted. So, then she asked, 'What is the answer? Why am I here then?' Much later in life, Veronica discovered John 3:16, 'For God so loved the world, that He gave His one and only Son, that whoever believes in Him should not perish, but have eternal life.'

Ephesians 1:3–5 reads: [3] Blessed be the God and Father of our Lord Jesus Christ, who has blessed us with every spiritual blessing in the heavenly places in Christ, [4] even as He chose us in Him before the foundation of the world, that we would be holy and without defect before Him in love, [5] having predestined us for adoption as children through Jesus Christ to Himself, according to the good pleasure of His desire.

Ephesians 1:11 states: 'We were also assigned an inheritance in Him, having been foreordained according to the purpose of Him who does all things after the counsel of His will.'

Veronica was content that she had found a place of peace and rest where, internally, she could flourish with ease, no longer striving but knowing that God had gifted her with every spiritual blessing.

MESSAGE TO THE READER

You are invited today to reflect and discuss how you can find more meaning and fulfilment in your life. This story encourages you not to settle for the surface level of your experiences. Instead, delve deeper within yourself and explore what else is available for your personal growth. This exploration has the potential to launch you into your true destiny.

Take control of your life situations and do not let others dictate your path. Ensure you are the one at the steering wheel of your journey. Conduct thorough research to understand your current position and determine the direction you need to take in life. You have been dealt a unique set of cards—how will you play them?

PRAYER

Father, bless each reader with the wisdom to seek You in all things, the courage to walk the path You have set before them, and the faith to trust in Your timing. May their hearts be open to Your calling, their minds renewed by Your Word, and their spirits refreshed by Your love.

As they reflect on the lessons shared within these pages, may they be reminded that they are chosen, loved, and predestined for greatness in Your Kingdom. Let their lives be a testament to Your glory, and may they carry the light of Your truth into the world.

Thank You Lord, for the opportunity to share this testimony. May it be a seed planted in fertile soil, bearing fruit for Your Kingdom. To You be all the honour, glory, and praise.

In Jesus' name, Amen.

ABOUT THE AUTHOR

Earlin Blair is a qualified Adult Social Worker from Manchester University with over 27 years of experience working with adults. Her expertise includes completing comprehensive assessments, managing and setting up support packages, serving as a telephonist and communicator in meetings, and holding qualifications as a Best Interest Assessor and Practice Educator.

She has delighted in receiving students from local universities, supporting them through their training, and witnessing their development over the duration of their placements. Her career has been life-changing and a privilege, providing the opportunity to meet many remarkable people and collaborate with other professionals. These experiences have been a time of personal growth, learning to invest in those around her, and accepting their love. She believes the world is a beautiful place with an abundance of goodness, and she is thankful to everyone who has been part of this journey of working and sharing skills.

Moving forward, she is a committed Citizen of the Kingdom of God. Her most recent calling has been to invest in children and youth, ensuring that the Body of Jesus will have generational influencers to carry the baton into the future.

REVIEW ASK

Thank you for reading this book. I sincerely hope that you have been equipped, encouraged, and inspired along the way. I would love to hear your comments on how this book has helped you. Please leave a review on Amazon.

Contact Details:

If you have been impacted by my book and would like to share your thoughts, I would love to hear from you.

Email: blairearlin@gmail.com

Printed in Great Britain
by Amazon

46081276R00056